Riding a Lion

Coral Rumble is an award winning and popular writer. In 2018 she won the Caterpillar Poetry Prize. She has worked as a poet and performer for many years and now specialises in writing and performing for children. Coral has three collections published, *Creatures, Teachers and Family Features, Breaking the Rules,* and *My Teacher's as Wild as a Bison*. Both of her later collections were featured in the 'Best Books' supplement of Junior Education Magazine and were selected as choices by the Children's Poetry Bookshelf. She has also contributed to around 150 anthologies for children. Coral performs and gives workshops at art centres, museums, bookshops, libraries, theatres and festivals, as well as in schools. Michael Rosen has commented, 'Rumble has a dash and delight about her work'.

Emily Ford is a freelance illustrator from Cumbria. From a young age she had a passion for storytelling and reading, which inspired her to create her own imaginary worlds populated with characters and magic. After studying for a degree in illustration she began working on children's books inspired by classic fairy tales and comics. Emily collaborated with her friend Stevie Westgarth to create *Aife and Stray: Seven Style Secrets for a Perilous Party* published by Troika in 2019. This is her third book for children.

Riding a Lion

Poems by Coral Rumble
Illustrations by Emily Ford

troika

*For my husband, John, who
always supports, always encourages,
and makes me believe I can ride lions!*

C. R.

Published by TROIKA

First published 2020

Troika Books Ltd
Well House, Green Lane, Ardleigh CO7 7PD
www.troikabooks.com

Text copyright © Coral Rumble 2020
Illustrations copyright © Emily Ford 2020

The moral rights of the
author and illustrator have been asserted

All rights reserved

A CIP catalogue record for this book
is available from the British Library

ISBN 978-1-912745-02-9

1 3 5 7 9 10 8 6 4 2

Printed in Poland

Contents

Introduction	9

Let Me Tell You a Story...

Riding a Lion	13
Once Upon a Time	14
Once Upon an Awful Time	15
On Why You Shouldn't Catch a Witch's Cackle	16
Disappointed Frog	17
One Shoe Tall, and Three Shoes Wide	18
Beyond Ariel	20
Dragon's Pride	22

All Creatures Great and Small

Proud Fox	24
Red Fox	25
Black Cat Remembers an Ancient Tale	26
It's a Small World	27
House Guest	28
Yak in the Attic	29
Neighbourhood Watch (Big Cat Style)	30
It's a King Thing	32
My Teacher Is a Bearded Dragon Lizard	33
Note to the Babysitter	35
8	36
The Climber	37
7 Out of 8	38
Field Exercises	39

A Sloth's Diary	40
Entrepreneur	42
Wrinkly Bottoms	43
Dave	44
Barn Owl	45
Sunrise Seagull	46

Any Time, Any Weather

Sunrise	48
Shift Work	49
White Space	50
A Sleepless Night	51
Bedtime	52
Dark	53
What Eye Am I?	54
North Pier, Blackpool	55
Squall	56

Out and About

Home Coming	59
School Coach Trip	60
The Art Police	61
The Rhythm of Ribs	62
The Librarian Doesn't Eat Children	63
Epitaph in a Shopping Mall	64
Epitaph in a Cinema Foyer	65
Raise a Toast to Tessa	66

Family and Feelings

Hugs and Kisses	68
Visiting Freddie	69
After the Storm	70
Didn't or Did	71
Staying Home	72
What Love Looks Like	73
Looking for Riley	74
Who She's Meant to Be	75
Fish Tale	76
Circus Clown	77
Rope Swing	78
Delicate Things	79
Cracks	80
The Lie Fox	81
Island	82
Spark	84

Getting Wordy

The Interrupting Full Stop	87
Cabbages	88
How High Can You Haiku?	90
Acrostics	91
Pantomime Poem	92
Rustle, Pitter-Patter, Trickle	94
Sounding You Out	95
Mammal Monthly – October Edition	96

Introduction

Life is a rollercoaster of ups and downs, so I wanted this collection of poems to follow the thrill of the track. Some days I laugh and some days I cry, and some days I think really, really hard. Many of these poems are about real life, others are about life as it is found only in my quirky imagination. Sometimes, you have to take risks in life, ride on a huge, flying lion and see where it takes you!

Between the covers of this book, you will find poems that puzzle you, tell you stories, make you ask questions. There will be dangerous poems, delicate poems and daft poems. One minute you'll be hiding in a dusty PE cupboard with a friend who is sad, the next you'll be buying an ice-cream from a polar bear! So, whether you're in a thinking mood, a sad mood, a laughing mood, or a crazy mood, I hope there are some poems within these pages that will match your mood, and keep you company.

Let Me Tell You a Story...

Riding a Lion

I dreamt of riding a lion, a fast one,
A fierce one, with a flash of wildness in his eyes.
I could feel his tented ribs with my clinging knees.

I dreamt he leapt and flew, huge wings spreading,
His deep growl rumbling like a well-oiled engine,
My fingers curled into a tangle around his mane.

I dreamt he swooped a deep dive, a daring dive,
A dizzy dive, against the roaring wind,
And I didn't even close my eyes in fear.

I dreamt he landed on an island, a golden one,
Where all the lions fly, and children ride
On their warm backs, clutching the edge of danger.

Once Upon a Time,

I turned the page of my storybook
And out he popped, with a wild look.
He prowled and growled, he snapped his jaws,
He flicked his sharp, white, slicing claws.
He tumbled down onto the floor
And trotted, lightly, to the door.

And through the window I could see
His amber eyes look back at me.
His ribs stood stiff beneath his coat,
His hair fluffed out around his throat.
Then, in a blink, I saw him running,
A lightning flash of speed and cunning.

He's gone to search for forest tracks
Where he can hide his grey-brown back,
But, now, how will the story scare
Without his cold and frightening stare,
Without his howling in the night,
Without his shadow in moonlight?

What creature has escaped from the storybook?

Once Upon an Awful Time

One day I cut my finger on the screech of a witch,
Fell from a beanstalk into a muddy, farmyard ditch.
Felt the prick of a spindle, and a wolf's jagged bite,
Looked into a cracked mirror, and got a dreadful fright.
I ate a rosy apple and got awful indigestion,
(There was poison deep inside, of that there is no question)
Got locked in a castle, and my heart missed a beat
When I heard the loud roar of a huge, snarling beast.
I ran to a cottage, inside there were three bears,
They wouldn't let me eat or sleep, or sit upon their chairs.
I saw a house of gingerbread, and a casket made of glass,
It all felt kind of spooky, so I quickly ran straight past.
I bandaged up the finger, cut on the witch's screech,
Then quickly found the exit, to put me safely out of reach.
And all because I saw a shiny poster on display: -
'Fairy-tale Land invites you to its special Open Day!'

On Why You Shouldn't Catch a Witch's Cackle

I caught a witch's cackle,
Put it in a storage jar,
It leapt around and scratched the sides
'Til the glass was scored and scarred.

It gibbered, chortled, clucked and crowed,
With its spiky, shrill, cold rasp,
It scraped and sliced with a witch's spite,
Until it broke the glass.

Disappointed Frog

I am a disappointed frog
With unrealised potential;
As a tadpole I was told
I would be influential.

But here I sit and croak,
My goggly eyes asquint,
Staring failure in the face –
I'll never be a prince!

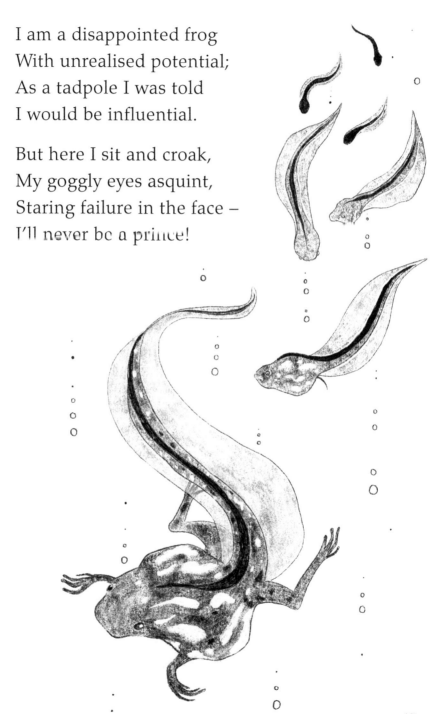

One Shoe Tall, and Three Shoes Wide

THE QUESTION

On the table is a box,
It has one handle and three locks,
Round its middle, a rope is tied,
It's one shoe tall, and three shoes wide.

If you touch the sides and lid
(Covering whatever's hid)
You'll feel a pulse, as your fingers glide
Over one shoe tall, and three shoes wide.

The hinges are the rusted sort,
Rigid, fixed, like a stubborn thought,
What's in this box, what does it hide?
It's one shoe tall, and three shoes wide.

Hold your breath, let thinking spill,
And listen hard as you stand still,
The box plays music deep inside,
It's one shoe tall, and three shoes wide.

THE ANSWER

On the table is a box,
It has one handle and three locks,
You'll hear my screechy song inside
This one shoe tall, and three shoes wide.

Touch the lid, and then explore,
You'll feel the pulsing of my roar
As it ascends and then subsides,
In one shoe tall, and three shoes wide.

Untie the rope and bust the locks,
Release me from this ancient box
Where, for centuries, I have sighed
In one shoe tall, and three shoes wide.

Then I'll spread my folded wings,
Screech and roar from deep within,
Mock one shoe tall, and three shoes wide
Who dared to catch a griffin's child.

Beyond Ariel

Beyond the rocks and shipwreck treasure,
A mermaid sits, she's tired and weathered,
Her grey hair splits with dry old age,
Her story's marked on the last page.

She lifts her threadbare tail in pain,
Her face is written with the strain
Of swimming, now the tide has turned,
And all she is, is all she's learned.

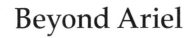

For the shifting sands of time have lulled
Her thoughts to slow, her beauty dulled,
And her song stays deep within her throat,
Every trembling, trailing note.

Because ancient tales of eternal youth
Are cruel lies, to hide the truth
That every mermaid has her day,
Then floats and fades and drifts away.

Dragon's Pride

Dragon has lost his fire.
Occasionally, a small spark leaks out
And dribbles down his chin,
Trickles into darkness.

Dragon has lost his fire.
The heat in his belly is from embers,
And the flicker on his tongue wanes
As he licks his wounds.

Dragon has lost his fire.
The last knight was skilled -
His sword sliced through scales
And punctured Dragon's pride.

Dragon has lost his fire.
His cave is black and bitter -
A lair for the vanquished,
A tomb for the legendary.

He stood by the wall, in its shadowy veil,
Where colours dissolve, mingle into a grey,
And his proud chest pushed into the stillness of night,
Rising and falling, his coat stretching tight.

And my gaze didn't falter, my eyes didn't blink,
As he caused me to wonder what proud foxes think
When they stand like they've brought us the moon's
   crystal light,
And bathe in the silver dew of a hushed night.

Red Fox

Red fox

    leaves a trail

    where he has stepped

        this snowy morning,

    leaving his

        frozen scent nesting

    in the holes

        of his paw
    prints.

Black Cat Remembers an Ancient Tale

Black Cat – inky, leaping shadow –
Lands on a wall cushioned with moss.
She sits, she stares, she waits,
Comfortable with her own company.

She looks at the moon and remembers a tale
About a cow jumping over it,
About a small dog laughing.
She muses on how a dog should never laugh,
About how dogs do not deserve happiness.
There was a cat in the ancient tale, though,
A brilliant cat of outstanding musical ability.
She recalls how a dish ran away with a spoon –
She doesn't know why, but the cat didn't get involved,
Which must mean it was an unimportant detail.

Black Cat's ears twitch, her sleek head turns
As a breeze pushes a parched leaf from the wall.
There's a smell of burnt hickory in the air, and
Over the wall, the church clock strikes 1.
Black Cat jumps, instinctively knows a mouse will run by.
The patterns of stories reside in her bones.

It's a Small World

The clownfish was a down fish,
He cried and cried and cried,
When he discovered the aquarium
Was just a tank inside.

He hid behind a plastic cave,
Attacked the weed and grass,
He sulked beside the filter pump,
And scowled into the glass.

The clownfish was a down fish,
Filled with raw emotion,
When he found he lived in Clapham
And not deep down in the ocean.

House Guest

There's a platypus in the bath,
Is someone having a laugh?
He's roped some sticks together
To make himself a raft.

He's floating by the overflow
And underneath the taps,
He's diving, periodically,
His feet go flip and flap.

He hasn't got much room,
He lacks essential space,
But he seems to have a smile
On his dopey, duck-billed face.

He doesn't seem too bothered
By the slip of the enamel,
He appears to rather like the feel
Of the softly folding flannel.

I don't know where he's come from,
I don't know why he's there,
But the next time that I need a bath
I won't much like to share!

Yak in the Attic

I was searching in the attic
When I found a dusty yak it
Raced around the back it
Was scared and made a racket.
It hid, I couldn't track it,
It must have thought I'd whack it
Or simply try to stack it,
Or find a box and pack it

Its fear was automatic,
When I found it, it stood static,
So I had a chance to vac it,
Which might seem a bit drastic.
But I never did attack it,
Or push or pull or smack it,
For I was really quite ecstatic –
To find a yak up in the attic!

Neighbourhood Watch*
(Big Cat Style)

Left right, left right,
See the sergeant-major with his stripes,
Left right, left right,
His fangs hang low like stalactites.
Quick march, legs swing,
About turn with a military spin,
Quick march, legs swing,
Flash goes the orange of his stripy skin.
Whiskers straight, lips coal-black,
This is a tiger that is never slack,
Whiskers straight, lips coal-black,
This is a tiger that watches his back.

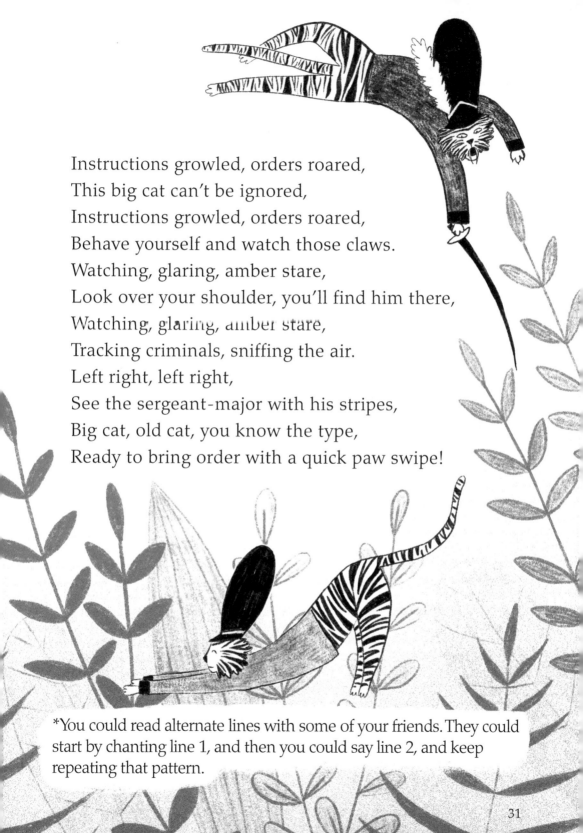

Instructions growled, orders roared,
This big cat can't be ignored,
Instructions growled, orders roared,
Behave yourself and watch those claws.
Watching, glaring, amber stare,
Look over your shoulder, you'll find him there,
Watching, glaring, amber stare,
Tracking criminals, sniffing the air.
Left right, left right,
See the sergeant-major with his stripes,
Big cat, old cat, you know the type,
Ready to bring order with a quick paw swipe!

*You could read alternate lines with some of your friends. They could start by chanting line 1, and then you could say line 2, and keep repeating that pattern.

It's a King Thing

Walk down the corridor,
And listen, if you're fearless,
To the strange noises coming
From the head teacher's office.
You might hear a growl,
You might hear a grrrr,
If you look through the keyhole,
You might see some fur.
You might hear a snap
As his desk breaks in two,
You might hear some scratching,
They say you often do.
You might detect sniffing
And the sound of crunching teeth,
You might hear curtains rip
And floorboards creak beneath.
Some say they've heard a thud
When he flops down on the floor,
Some say a scary shadow leaks
From underneath the door.
His laws must not be broken,
He rules with a rod of iron -
Discipline's no problem
When the head teacher's a lion!

My Teacher is a Bearded Dragon Lizard

My teacher is a bearded dragon lizard,
He's friendly, in a prickly sort of way,
He strides around the playground every break time,
His designer stubble always on display.

He teaches us about the desert plains
And about the lands where people walk through blizzards;
He teaches us about the rocks and plants,
And when it comes to maths, well, he's a wizard!

When we have PE, he winks his eye,
As he demonstrates some lizard climbing tricks,
Then balances along a slanting branch,
Before he gives his scaly tail a flick.

At lunchtime he relaxes in the sun,
He basks upon a rock and drinks his tea.
Sometimes he eats a cricket sandwich snack,
Then stretches in the heat, so wild and free.

But story time is when he's at his best;
He tells us tales of creatures bold and brave,
And when he gets excited his head bobs,
And his skinny little arms give frantic waves.

My teacher is a bearded dragon lizard
And we all behave for him so he will stay,
When your teacher is a bearded dragon lizard
You wouldn't have it any other way.

Note to the Babysitter

Ignatius our iguana
Is roaming in the hall,
He likes to climb the stairs
He likes to scale the wall.
He rests up on the curtain rod,
So please don't get a shock,
And sometimes he will drape himself
Over the kitchen clock.

Ignatius our iguana
Just loves to entertain,
He'll sit upon your lap
If you dare to call his name.
His claws look pretty scary,
Being long and thin,
But you'll have a friend for life
If you stroke his little chin.

Ignatius our iguana
Is free to run and climb,
You'll often catch a glimpse
Of a ridge of dorsal spines.
He might look like a dragon,
He might appear to glare,
But Ignatius our iguana
Would never want to scare.

(Be back at 10. Help yourself to drinks)

8*

Amid the cluttered corner of a living room,
Resting in the shadow of a sofa cushion,
A miniature monster waits to perform as
Carnival stilt-walker, cloaked in dark horror.
His eight eyes focus, his eight legs tense.
Nobody can predict his path, or his intention.
Icy fear spreads and grips as you notice the
Deliberate flexing of legs. Can you feel the phobia?

*Clue: Can you spell well?

The Climber

See him climbing up the wall,
Step by step I watch him crawl,
Leg by leg he feels his way
Through the shadows of the day.
At the ceiling he will stop,
Cast his threads and start to drop
Down and down, he knows no failure,
Expert climber and abseiler.

7 Out of 8

See the hobbling spider
Struggling up the wall,
Cup your hands beneath him,
He's just about to fall.
For 7 of his legs
Co-ordinate his course,
But he has to swing leg number 8
With all his spider force.
For spiders lag behind
In prosthetic engineering*,
But in website building,
They have been pioneering.

*Prosthetic engineering is the making of body bits to replace the parts that have worn out, or are broken. In this case, spiders have tried to replace the spider's leg. They need a bit of practise!

Field Exercises

Beat of the Sheep

Bleat, bleat, bleat, goes the beat of the sheep,
As they huddle up together like a fluffy white sheet,
As they nuzzle and squash and jostle by the wall,
And sing out together their baa baa call.

Bleat, bleat, bleat, go the white and the black,
As the field mist washes their woolly sheep backs,
As they stare at each other with vacant eyes,
Happy to avoid any kind of exercise.

Billy

In the garden stands a goat,
But you can call him Billy,
He's munching washing on a line,
So his mouth looks pink and frilly.
He's always hungry, never full,
His waistline is expanding,
His idea of exercise
Is staring hard while standing.

A Sloth's Diary

MONDAY:
To do –

Climb tree
Cling to trunk of tree
Sit in fork of tree
Hang upside down
from tree

Sleep –
Do it
tomorrow

TUESDAY:
To do –

Climb tree
Cling to trunk of tree
Sit in fork of tree
Hang upside down
from tree

Sleep –
Do it
tomorrow

WEDNESDAY:

To do –

Climb tree
Cling to trunk of tree
Sit in fork of tree
Hang upside down
from tree

Sleep –
Do it
tomorrow

THURSDAY:

To do –

Climb tree
Cling to trunk of tree
Sit in fork of tree
Hang upside down
from tree

Entrepreneur

Polar bear ices,
Brilliant prices,
A lolly to lick
At the end of a stick.
No ordinary van
Staffed by a man,
Instead, a white bear
Fluffing his hair,
And huge polar paws
With sharp polar claws.
The master of cool,
He's nobody's fool;
He prefers polar
To anything solar.
Come near to savour
Each polar bear flavour,
He fills every cone
With a style of his own
(It was something to do,
On escaping the zoo).
The locals all stare
But he doesn't care;
He's an entrepreneur
All covered in fur.

Wrinkly Bottoms

It's a rainy day and the elephant house
Is bursting at the seams,
It's full of tusks and trunks and ears
And elephantine screams.

Peggy polishes her tusks
And Casper plays guitar,
Grimble snoozes by the wall
And Wellington plays cards.
Boo pokes shoulders, pinches thighs,
To get herself more room,
And Frizzell's sighs of boredom
Just increase the sombre gloom.
Dunstan tells an ancient joke
And Winston makes a groan,
Hilda does what she does best,
She moans and moans and moans!
Matilda does a crossword
And Lulu hums a tune,
They tap their nails and hope and pray
It will stop raining soon.

It's a rainy day and the elephant house
Is packed with wrinkly bottoms,
It's crammed with bulky body bits
And the smell is mighty rotten!

Dave

With a splash and a dash
And a certain panache,
He dives through the water to save,
With his teeth white and clean
He is every girl's dream,
The swimming pool lifeguard, called Dave.

He's dynamic and lean,
You know what I mean,
His back arches out like a bow,
He goes zigging and zagging,
With no hint of bragging,
He's the master of 'go with the flow'.

His tail flips and splashes,
His fin cuts deep gashes
In water, when he hears the alarm,
He's a rescue machine,
He's got James Bond genes
And a huge helping of natural charm.

He's so agile and quick,
His movements are slick,
He's water-resistant and brave,
So well-groomed and trim
With a Hollywood grin,
This dolphin is special, he's Dave!

Barn Owl

Barn owl, golden brown
With the ghostly sheen
Of an Elizabethan queen.
Long-legged claw curler,
Her flattened face turns
Like a satellite dish,
Her hooked beak shreds her call
Into a ragged screech.
She stands, watching shadows join,
Listening to the woody creak of beams.
Soon she will lock onto a foraging mouse
Then sweep through the air
Like a spectre's feathered aura,
Whispering her arrival and departure.

Sunrise Seagull

Sunrise seagull, up with the lark,
Ink tipped angel in the gilded sky,
Slicing sunrays as he swoops.
Flap and glide, flap and glide, spiralling up,
Sweeping the sky of lingering stars.
Plunging down and down to skim golden ripples,
Searching for a flash of fish tail,
As waves flip over like shaken bed sheets,
And Neptune rises to greet the day.

Sunrise

There's sunrise in the garden,
There's sunrise in the hall,
There's sunrise in the kitchen
Chasing shadows from the wall,

And light is snagging darkness
On specks of shiny dew,
That soak our shoes and socks
With a special kind of new.

There's sunrise in my cereal
And sunrise on my toast,
Of all the parts of every day,
It's sunrise I like most.

Shift Work
(A poem with no ending)

Morning stirs,
Throws back the duvet,
Squeezes through curtain cracks
And into people's lives.
He meets up with Sun,
Wipes his dewy brow,
Warms up, relaxes,
No hurry to meet Afternoon.
                        But Afternoon enters,
                        Bold as a brass band,
                        Playing his music of
                        Rush and catch up,
                        And Sun starts to hide
                        Behind the tall buildings,
                        Until Afternoon hears
                        The footsteps of Night.
And Night slips in quietly,
No big announcement,
And lights up car headlights
And the lamp posts of town,
She breathes out a slumber
Through cracks in the curtains,
Plumps up the duvet,
Waits for Morning to stir.
(Return to verse 1)

White Space

The moon is singing in my room,
He's chased away the night-time gloom,
He's thrown a veil of ivory gauze
Over my bed and desk and drawers.

My mirror flashes silver-bright,
The gentle sheen of frosted light,
I stretch, I yawn, I turn and curl,
Slip into sleep as white as pearl.

A Sleepless Night

A herd of dreams rushed through my mind,
You know the sort, the restless kind,
And every dream, within the herd
Made sure imagination stirred.

They stomped around inside my skull,
Each leaving me a thought to mull,
And then stampeded to my heart
To wake me with a sudden start.

Then, without warning of their flight,
They raced away into the night,
And I was left awake in bed,
A million questions in my head.

Bedtime
Cefalu Beach, Sicily

Fishing boats line up on shore -
They've done so many times before -
Weathered by the sea and sand,
Calmly resting on the land.

Nets are drying, oars are still,
The evening sunshine starts to spill
Over the sides of paint-cracked hulls
That sigh beneath the circling gulls.

Gentle ripples stroke their sterns
As evening sets the tide to turn,
And, in the glow of harbour lights,
They close their eyes and say goodnight.

Dark

It's dark in the park,
Despite the moon's glow,
As dark as the compost
That makes new seeds grow,
And the colours are fading,
Their shades turned down low,
Like the details of memories
From a long time ago.

It's dark in the park,
Despite stars in the sky,
And the swing that swung children
Can no longer fly,
And the tall, curving slide
Now looks recklessly high,
And the noise of the day
Shrivels into a sigh.

It's dark in the park,
Despite the lamplight,
And the limb-stretching trees
Are picking a fight
With the strengthening wind
That spits raindrops, with spite,
While an oil slick of shadows
Floods the hollow of night.

What Eye Am I*

It's the eye that stares,
The eye that silently follows
The swirl of its coat,
The eye that focuses on
Circling dust particles,
The eye that never squints,
Never blinks, stays steady,
And glides, as its gritty hair
Spins round and round,
It's the eye with tunnel vision.

*Puzzle it out
Answer: The eye of a storm

North Pier, Blackpool*

A single seagull circles overhead
And sea spray coats conservatory walls;
We huddle in the shelter, all hopes dead,
The wind is sharp, the waves stand strong and tall.
The carousel outside has lost its smile,
Its colours run in raindrop-coated air,
And deckchairs flap alone, in one long file,
Children fidget, adults sigh and stare
The distant arcade noise of ping and clank
Soon beckons every damp and soggy soul;
We drip along the creaky decking planks
To post a coin, or shoot, or stoop to bowl.
    And yet, despite the moping on this pier,
    We'll all return to shelter here next year!

*A sonnet

Squall

The engine hums,
The wipers squeak,
And lamplight flickers
On my cheek.

The indicators
Tap a path,
Occasionally,
I hear Dad laugh.

Dark clouds race
Across the moon
One star peeps through
A screen of gloom.

The night has turned
The sky to ink,
But in the warmth
I dream and think.

Raindrops slide,
My eyelids fall,
I doze and quit
The night-time squall.

Out and About

Home Coming

The beat of the train,
The glide of the track,
The rhythm of travel
Plays right down my back.
The speed of the fields,
The blur of the trees,
The flash of each tunnel
Paints pictures for me.
The clickerty-clack,
The line of the rails,
Speed me past houses
That could tell me tales.
The faces that frown,
The faces that smile,
Are joined in this carriage
Today, for a while.
The strangers who talk
The ones on the phone
Look forward to reaching
The shelter of home.

School Coach Trip

I'm not sitting next to Olivia,
I gossip about her to Ruth;
I'm not sitting next to Amanda,
She says that I don't tell the truth;
I'm not sitting next to Rebecca,
She thinks she's so cool in her coat;
I'm not sitting next to Daniella,
Beth showed her the note that I wrote;
I'm not sitting next to Camilla,
She's just not the popular sort;
I'm not sitting next to Fiona,
She'll want to share sweets that I've brought;
I'm not sitting next to Roxanna,
She's boring and far, far too shy,
And they say they'd rather not sit next to me,
I can't, for a moment, think why.

The Art Police

I walk slowly, counting my steps.
The gallery is large and important.
Famous paintings echo the voices of masters,
Some of the paint smells of history.
Huge frames cradle portraits;
Eyes stare out, follow me as I walk.
In another room, crazy brush strokes
Race across canvas without restraint,
Singing a colourful laughter.
My footsteps tap by sculptures.
I would like to touch the smooth surfaces
And trace, with my fingers, every angle,
But the art police are looking.
They stand, with legs apart and hands clasped,
Ready to pounce on children rude enough
To steal the dust of masterpieces.

The Rhythm of Ribs

The stethoscope man is on his rounds,
Doing the job he loves best;
He'll raise up the end like an elephant's trunk
And check out the beat of my chest.

The stethoscope man is on his rounds,
The rhythm of ribs makes him grin;
His patients play out the patterns of life,
Like iPods all covered with skin.

The Librarian Doesn't Eat Children

The librarian doesn't eat children,
It's a rumour I spread without thought,
She's partial to cheese, ham and tuna,
She's partial to cod, freshly caught,
She's partial to soup, beans and bacon,
She's partial to carrots and swede,
She's partial to pizza and pancakes,
She's partial to sesame seeds.
But the librarian doesn't eat children,
It's a lie that grew bigger than planned,
Go on, have a look, and borrow a book,
She won't even nibble your hand!

Epitaph in a Shopping Mall

Here lie the bones of William Potts,
Last seen trudging around the shops.
In trying hard to please his wife,
He prematurely ended life.
His wife comes daily to lay flowers –
And then shops on for hours and hours.

Epitaph in a Cinema Foyer

Here lies the body of film buff Rex,
He lived his life for special effects.
He's buried in this foyer, please excuse the mound,
It's the nearest we could get him to the Dolby sound.
He's now a silent movie, a picture without motion,
This poem is a tribute to his years of devotion.

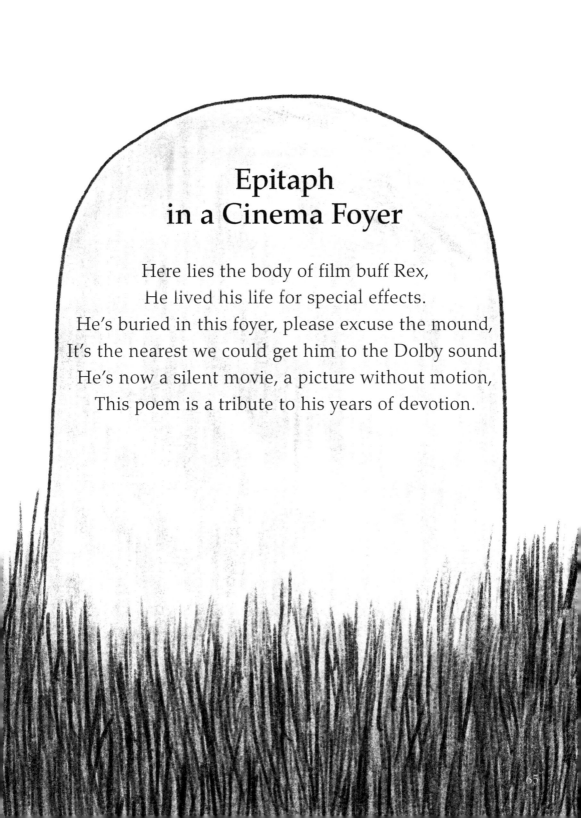

Raise a Toast to Tessa*

Tessa tested toasters
For the top toaster store,
Of the toasters Tessa tested,
Some toasters tested poor.

The other toasters toasted toast
To toasted toast perfection –
The store praises Tessa's testing
For a top toaster selection.

*A tongue twister

Family and Feelings

Hugs and Kisses*

At Aunty Gwenda's house the air is still,
The windows are shut tight, the doors are locked.
She hides away with too much time to fill,
When Uncle Billy died her world was rocked.
We visit every Tuesday, after school,
We take her fish and chips, a sort of treat.
We leave her house at 7, as a rule,
There's nothing left to say after we eat.
Mum says she is a prisoner of grief,
I think that means her sadness is locked in.
When death stole Uncle Billy, like a thief,
It left her with a life that's cold and thin.
    We give her hugs and kisses at the door,
    Perhaps that's what our Tuesday nights are for.

*A sonnet

Visiting Freddie

The ward, itself, is warmer than a womb,
Every bed is edged with flowers and smiles.
Tiny plastic cribs are wheeled around;
Here, it seems, that time rests for a while.

Mum is fast asleep upon her bed,
I kiss her satin cheek and stroke her hair,
I glance towards the crib right by her side,
And, sure enough, my brother's sleeping there.

His elfin nose is perfectly positioned,
His tiny fingernails are smooth and fine;
His lips compress into a baby kiss,
I whisper in his ear, 'You're mine, you're mine.'

After the Storm*

The bedroom door slams,
Sent to my room once again,
All shouting has stopped.
I reflect in the mirror –
Don't like what I see today.

Footsteps on the stairs,
A knock on the door, a pause.
Mum enters and sits.
Our hearts melt in the silence,
Our eyes cry a thousand words.

*Both verses are in Tanka verse form (extended Haiku, with two extra 7 syllable lines)

Didn't or Did*

When I'm caught out and angry, and tears start to flow,
I pack up my rucksack and quickly I go
To the huge, towering oak tree, in the field by the woods,
Where nobody says that I shouldn't or should.

I unpack my bag, spread my blanket and sit;
Feel the tree's cooling shadow, and hide under it.
I watch the birds fly through the branches that span
The space where no voice says I can't or I can.

My back rests against the deep patterns of bark,
And soon the sun makes an exchange with the dark,
Then I leave with clear thoughts that I gained as I hid
With a tree that's not bothered if I didn't or did.

*Have you got a special place you go to, when you're in trouble at home?

Staying Home

I look out of the lounge window.
Other school children walk by,
Weighed down by books and bags and bragging.
It's a short walk to school from here,
But it seems a million miles from home.
They'll be arriving now – the early birds
Keen for book learning and approving smiles.
They'll stand, shoulder to shoulder,
Glued together by their secrets,
And discuss yesterday's French test.
Ten minutes later the others will arrive,
Flexing muscles, strutting through the gate.
They'll stand, shoulder to shoulder,
Share their jokes and gum. Glare.
I usually leave for school when the bell has gone,
When the yard is empty of friend clusters.
But, today, I'm staying home with mum,
Who doesn't quite believe I have a stomach ache.

What Love Looks Like

That moment
When you've gone missing,
And the clock gets stuck
On a second,
And they call
Your friends
Who haven't seen you,
And nothing matters
But your empty bedroom.

That moment
When they see you,
And breath rushes
Back into their lungs,
So they can cry
And hug you
And tell you
How dark
Their fear was.

Looking for Riley

Riley had dragged the emptiness to school.
It would seem wrong to leave it in his bedroom
Where he had filled silent spaces with sobs.
Grandma had gone, but her songs hung in the air,
Small memories, pockets of comfort.

And now, in a dusty corner of the PE cupboard,
Riley sat and rocked and clutched his knees,
Resting his chin on his shiny, worn trousers
Stretching over his bent legs, hiding away
From questions he'd be asked, but couldn't answer.

They were all looking for Riley, the teachers, Mrs Moore.
They would try to wipe his grief away, catch his tears
Before they hit the ground, before they made a mark
In the dust, before they stopped falling of their own accord.
So, I hid with him, and somehow, it made him smile.

Who She's Meant to Be

A nervous star, up in the sky,
Felt anxious that she hung so high
While dreaming thickened in the air,
And even grown-ups climbed the stairs.

She didn't like the sky's dark hue
That cloaked her panoramic view,
She missed white clouds, she missed the sun
To hide behind 'til day was done.

And every night she closed her eyes,
Trembling, wishing for disguise;
She feared that if she once looked down,
She'd tumble to the sea and drown.

A nervous star, up in the sky,
Felt anxious that she hung so high,
Made every twinkle hard to see,
Denying who she's meant to be.

Fish Tale*

He was a common carp –
No class, disgusting habits!
Thick-skinned and leathery,
He pouted between barbels at passing fish,
Was made speechless by their mix of colours.
Brown, very brown, a common brown,
Hanging under a depressed dorsal fin.
He could be defined as 'ordinary'.
Accepting of his station,
He had scaled down his future plans –
Decided brown was enough for him.
He was not a fish to be moved
To finer feelings, higher aspirations;
Not the kind of fish to dream
Beyond his pond.

*A common carp is a widespread, brown, freshwater fish.
Barbels look like whiskers, near the mouth of the fish.

Circus Clown*

The hurdy-gurdy circus music drones,
A clown prepares to balance on a chair,
He hides behind a painted smile of stone.

The circus once was in his blood and bones,
But lately he's grown tired of the glare;
The hurdy-gurdy circus music drones.

He dresses in a caravan, alone,
His stripy suit shows signs of wear and tear,
He hides behind a painted smile of stone.

The chilling wind of loneliness has blown,
It has silenced hope that once hung in the air;
The hurdy-gurdy circus music drones.

Reflected in the mirror is a clone,
His clowning has become a cruel snare,
He hides behind a painted smile of stone.

He must perform, although his spirit groans,
He must amuse with sparkle, wit and flair;
The hurdy-gurdy circus music drones,
He hides behind a painted smile of stone.

*A villanelle

Rope Swing

He swings the rope,
Prepares to drop,
The river beckons
For the plop,
But fingers lock
Around the rope,
His gripping slipping,
With his hope.
All eyes watching,
Rhythmic voices
Tease and taunt,
Limit his choices,
And deep in the chant
There's nowhere to hide,
And deep in his heart
Is the pressure of pride.

Delicate Things

In the early stillness of the day,
I felt the sharpness of a ray
Of sun, that cut its way through mist
And scraped my arm, down to the wrist.

With wary fingers, I clasped it tight,
Snapped off a metre of its light,
Its glow was bright and sabre-sharp,
As thin as a string from an angel's harp.

I wrapped a cloth around one tip,
So I could cup my hand and grip
One end, then point it to the sky,
And gaze at it with squinting eyes.

Then swooping down, as with a sword,
I raced it through the air towards
The dry, cracked mud, the thinning grass –
It shattered like the finest glass.

In the early stillness of the day,
I couldn't find a word to say,
The fragments dulled, I felt the sting
Of disregard for delicate things.

Cracks

After an argument,
I assemble the broken pieces
Of conversation,
And fit them together.

There are always bits missing;
Syllables that flew too quickly,
Like sleek darts of hurt.

And, in my head,
I form the puzzle,
So I can look at the pieces,
Notice the cracks in my friendship.

The Lie Fox

Sometimes, the Lie Fox
Races out of my mouth
Before I can stop him.

He's a sneaky character -
Crafty, cunning, conniving,
Tricking my tongue into action.

Speedily, he darts into ears,
Wriggles into the minds
Of my trusting friends.

He's sly, that artful Lie Fox,
Always prising open my pursed lips,
Chasing the truth into dark corners.

Island

The boy, over there,
Is as silent as air,
He sits like a castaway
On his red classroom chair.

I'd like to cross over
The line that's been drawn
By Liam and Lucas,
By Aiden and Shaun,

But if I step onto
The island and talk,
They'll watch every move,
Every step that I walk,

Then Liam and Lucas
And Aiden and Shaun,
Will flash angry eyes
To threaten and warn.

So, the boy over there,
Who's as silent as air,
Will still sit marooned
On his red classroom chair,

And the sea of my guilt
Will crash in my ears,
As I drown in the swell
Of my worry and fears.

Spark

My red balloon escapes, like a giant spark,
Above smoky wisps,
Above the spit and hiss
Of the park bonfire.

I stare up, search with my eyes
While my ears fill with the crackle
Of sapless twigs and dusty branches.
My face is tinged with firelight,
I blink the dryness away.

A girl walks by, with a red balloon,
Holding tightly to the string.
A spark flickers inside me,
Coals of jealously glow.

The Interrupting Full Stop

Once there was a full stop,
As heavy as a rock,
He was never happy
'Til a flow of words had stopped.

He rolled up to each sentence,
Stared right into its eyes –
It always took the letters
Completely by surprise.

He captured words and hemmed them in,
Broke colons clean in half,
He folded semicolons
To leave a dot, and then he laughed –

'I am the king of page and book,
No letter can get past,
When your ideas flood the page
I'll be the dam across their path.

'I rule each story that you write,
I dictate your punctuation,
I'll stop your moving train of thought,
Like a buffer at a station.'

Cabbages

(A poem for your teacher to read aloud)

How do we know that words mean their meanings
And who decided their fate?
How do we know that large isn't small
And that bricks build a wall not a gate?

How do we know that the sky is the sky
And not really ground, grass or land?
How do we know that a wreck is a mess
And not a construction well-planned?

How do we know that begin's the beginning
And why do we call it the start?
 How do we know that a whole is a whole
And not, on reflection, a part.

How do we know that a word is a word
And not just a letter instead?
How do we know that a sentence makes sense
And that scanning it, constitutes read?

How know do we that a bull is a bull
And not a canal or a tree?
Do and know we how that a hill is a hill
And not an excitable flea?

How know we do a that chair is a chair
not And a table or door?
do know how we And that our feet come to rest
On a permanent fixture called floor?

poem How that a we know a do poem's
just muddle sound a And of not?
do a that mad gone poet's how we And know,
That lost sanity's found his and not?

Can you work out the correct word order in the last 3 verses? Why do you think I muddled them up? Who do you think decided what words mean?

How High Can You Haiku?

Hai hai hai hai hai
And up, and over, and down,
Ku ku ku ku ku!

Acrostics

Acrostics
Clearly
Reveal
Obsessional
Selection
Tendencies
In
Clever
Sequencing

Pantomime Poem*

I'm going to write a pantomime poem
OH NO YOU'RE NOT!
Oh yes I am!
One that will get everyone going
OH NO YOU'RE NOT!
Oh yes I am!

They'll be huge custard pies
And girls who slap thighs,
Men dressed in frocks
And bloomers with dots,
They'll be beanstalks and castles,
Some heroes, some rascals.
They'll be goodies to sing to
And villains BEHIND YOU!
They'll be eggs that are golden,
An actor who's an olden!
Cows all called Daisy
And songs that are crazy!

I'm going to write a pantomime poem
OH NO YOU'RE NOT!
Oh yes I am!
One that will get everyone going
OH NO YOU'RE NOT!
Oh yes I am!
OH NO YOU'RE NOT!
Oh yes I am!
OH NO YOU'RE NOT!
I just did!!

*Let your friends be your audience, and play their part!

Rustle, Pitter-Patter, Trickle

In my bag of gentle sounds,
I'll place soft words, downy and round,
Words that never cut or slice,
Words as smooth as polished ice.

I'll start with feather, whisper, ripple,
Rustle, pitter-patter, trickle,
I'll drop in murmur, shell and sea,
Then fur, sing, sail, along with bee.

And when the world around me jangles,
As people speak words with sharp angles,
I'll open the drawstring, let syllables fly,
Disarm spite's shout with the wisp of a sigh.

Sounding You Out*

Onomatopoeia,
Wouldn't want to be yer,
Banging, crashing, hooting,
Where soft words cannot steer.

Onomatopoeia,
Don't even have to see yer;
I can hear you bark and buzz
Filling gentle words with fear.

Onomatopoeia,
So long, farewell, and see yer,
Unless you whisper, 'shush' and 'hush',
To calm the atmosphere.

*Onomatopoeic words sound like the thing they describe. We tend to notice the loud sounding words more than the soft ones. They're such bullies!

MAMMAL MONTHLY
October Edition Advertisements
PROPERTY TO LET

FEMALE rabbit required to share 2-bedroom hutch.
Fully furnished with hay and newspaper.
Low ceiling – hopping height restriction.
Non-smoker.
No pets.
75 carrots per month, all bills included.

SPACIOUS kennel to let, in quiet neighbourhood.
Set in beautiful garden away from busy road, allowing for off-road barking.
Enough room to swing a cat.
No slobbering.
150 bones per month.

IMMACULATE 1-bedroom hamster cage,
set in cat-free living room, furnished to high standard.
Would suit tidy female, prone to excessive hoarding.
Personal gym includes treadmill wheel.
Nocturnal habits tolerated.
75 pieces of dried fruit per month.

WELL-PRESENTED, semi-detached mouse hole, near to local amenities, eg. fridge, larder.
No drive. Restricted entry.
A slim figure necessary.
Ideal for a family or professional sharers.
Squeaking hours negotiable.
Gnawing discouraged.
80 cheese slices per month.